Table of Contents

Introduction

This manual is for restaurant management, greeters and waitstaff. Managers need to be trained and master every position in your restaurant. If there is a call out or if sales is more than expected, management needs to jump in and help reduce the stress in whatever position that is falling behind.

This manual is also for waitstaff and greeters. This manual will give you detailed information on how to train your employee's in operational excellence and WOW customer service.

Training is an Investment not an Expense. Many restaurant owners and managers look at training as an expense rather than an investment.

59% of restaurants fail in the first 3 years. 26% the first year, 19% fail the second year and 14% fail the 3rd year. These are very scary statistics, this leaves no room for error, do it right the first time.

Training is not just to survive, it is to maintain a balance in which you can excel and conquer!

Training has been a part of everyone's life throughout time. Years ago, a young teenage boy would begin his training with an experienced mentor who knew the business. Without the proper training we all would be lost and broke. Training your employees is one of the smartest moves you can make your business successful. If people are not trained, how would we expect them to know the job or to do it correctly?

If you are putting your money and time into your work, then you want to make that an investment and not a gamble. The businesses that are surviving must be doing something right. Do you really want to lose your money in a gamble by going into a business with no training or tools, or do you want to invest your money into something that will lead you to profits?

Many people invest and open a restaurant and don't have the knowledge to make it succeed. The goal of this book is to give you guidance and tools to be prosperous in your business.

I really don't think anyone wants to fail; most of us dream of becoming successful. You need to do more than just dream, you need to take your time and think it out and plan it correctly.

Introduction

I am about to tell you of my personal experience. It was a tough road for me and I really did not know what I wanted to do. My wife told me quite often that in 2012 we will have our own business. Every time she said that to me, all I could think was, 'How is that going to happen?' She also said that it has to be something you really want to do and sometimes that is so much a "part of you" that you don't even realize that other people don't have that gift.

I wondered what I could do. I did a lot of research and there was one consistent comment most people said, "Do what you love." My wife pointed out to me that everything I do and say is about the restaurant business. I often refer to our home pantry as "dry storage" or our refrigerator as a "walk-in." For me, it's the Restaurant Business and I have been in it for over 25 years.

I love the business, I love being around people and the challenges that every day brings. I know it like the back of my hand. I have always been a company man, I have been through several management training courses, although most of my experience came from on the job experience.

I believe in doing the right thing and applying common sense. I was fortunate to have worked with really great people; I was trained the right way and stuck to it consistently every day.

In this Management Training Manual I have developed ways to help you gain success in your business. If you are just starting a business or just thinking about it, this will definitely be beneficial for you.

This manual explains step-by-step instructions in training management, waitstaff and greeter job descriptions to guide you in training your employees.

This manual gives you an understanding of how a restaurant should operate. A successful restaurant takes a lot of dedication on everyone's part. Much of the success of the restaurant is upon the Owner or General Manager. This person is a key player and oversees everything.

Other key roles are the restaurant managers and supervisors who run the shifts from day to day. A thriving business will have well trained leaders who are consistent among each other. Visualize a chain with links, and each link is a workplace leader.

Now visualize that the chains run a machine, what happens when you twist a wrench into the chains when the machine is running; it is most likely going to stop. Just like the engine, if the management team is not consistently promoting the same things, then the chain will be twisted up or broken and everything stops.

Managers learn correct policies, procedures and how the different position function and how to keep it going in the right direction. The Managers make sure everything they learned is consistently occurring from day to day. To ensure the system works the General Manager or the owner oversees the rest of the management.

Waitstaff will be learning the six steps of service from beginning to end. These steps are very important in ensuring that your guest receive exceptional service. The very minute your guest enter the restaurant is when the first step begins. As long as the servers are working the steps consistently and correctly, you and the guest will reap the benefits. Of course, managers and supervisors will have to monitor the servers to ensure that the six steps of service are occurring from shift to shift.

Introduction

In addition, each crew member needs to be trained correctly. For the best results one or two certified trainers need to responsible for the training. If you are going to train someone and spend the money for it, then it is best to do right the first time. This manual will teach people, whether they possess experience or no experience in the food service industry. Easy to understand step by step instructions with clear understanding of all topics outlined in this manual. This is one of the most important positions to set the tone for the correct procedures that need to be installed in all employees.

In order for the training process to be effective the trainers need to be selected by the following criteria:

- Consistency in following all established policies and procedures.
- Mature in age and in doing the right thing for the right reasons.
- Takes criticism well and uses it toward correcting the issue.
- Respects all other employees, including the management team.
- Does not follow the crowd, but sticks to what is correct.
- Position knowledge and execution above standard.
- Has the best interest of the restaurant in mind.
- Has a passion for keeping the business profitable.
- Knows the importance of high quality customer service.

It is recommended to promote this person into the position as trainer if possible. If you do not have a certified trainer, then it is recommended to use a manager with the qualities noted above. You cannot afford to let a non-qualified trainer train your employees. I have been in the business for years and I have seen inadequate training occur in over 75% in the cases.

The worst thing you can do is to let an inexperienced or poorly trained employee train a new person. In my experience, it is an unfortunate event that often occurs; an employee with bad habits or poor training teaches incorrect information to the new staff members. Training is very costly, and you cannot afford to keep hiring, training and losing employees.

This is a domino effect-the non-qualified employee trained someone incorrectly, and the bad habits continue to be passed on as new staff come in. The new person who is poorly trained gets frustrated and either quit or continues the incorrect behavior. This is often referred to as a "rotating door."

As a tool to help you keep the restaurant in the above average area I would encourage you to empower the trainers to be able to correct any employee that are not following procedures or policies whether they are training or not training.

Think of it as a second pair of eyes. To take it further, invite them to participate in the manager meetings. This gives the trainers a strong sense of support and they know their job is an important role in the team. The trainers can give excellent input on issues that may be occurring in the restaurant.

Consistency is the Key to your Restaurant's Success

It has been said time and time again that consistency creates success. But if it's really as easy as it sounds, why aren't all restaurant owners wildly successful?

Think back to a time in your life when you achieved some form of success – whether it was in academics, in sports or in business. Maybe you aced a big exam, winning a particular trophy, or exceeding a sales target.

In the time leading up to that successful moment, you most likely made an intentional decision to commit yourself to achieving that goal. Perhaps you studied every day for a week before the exam. Or regularly trained with your team before the big game. You were determined to remain consistently persistent and do whatever it took to win.

So what's stopping you from applying that same diligence and determination into your daily routine today?

In this manual certain information will be repetitive. For, example, some information in the server training area maybe be duplicated in another area in this manual. The reason for this is we want you to retain the information by memory.

The information that was gathered to create this manual was from individuals that worked in the restaurant industry, specifically corporate restaurants for over 25 years.

"It's not what we do once in a while that shapes our lives, but what we do consistently."
Tony Robbins

"We are what we repeatedly do. Excellence, then, is not an act, but a habit."
Aristotle

Orientation
Orientation Paperwork

Before a manager, supervisor or key-holder is hired it might be a really great idea to do a thorough background check, job reference check, personal finances check and drug test.

The person you hire as a manager, supervisor or key-holder will be handling money and sensitive material. Know who you are hiring before you hire.

Before you hire any employee you should do a thorough previous job reference check. Do the interview first, and then do a job reference check. When doing a reference check match up the reference check to the application and interview for consistent information.

If you do not do a reference check on your employees, you are risking everything. Do you know who you are hiring? The last thing you need is an employee who is dishonest and non-performing. This will also create a rotating door of employees who are either terminated or an employee who quit.

This route can be very expensive, it is best to do the right thing and do the reference check to avoid the loss of time and money.

Before the first day of training begins, the paperwork and orientation must be completed.

Paperwork consists of the following

- Completely filled out Job application.
- W-4: Go to this website to print out a W-4 www.irs.gov/pub/irs-pdf/fw4.pdf
- I-9: Go to this website to print out a I-9 www.uscis.gov/files/form/i-9.pdf
- Work permits (See the below pages for PA minor laws).

__Always refer to your own State laws regarding paperwork, minor laws and wages.__

On the next page are topics to go over with your employees. These Orientation topics are more common in most restaurants.

Orientation
Orientation Topics and Information

The Instructor's Background

Use this time to introduce yourself as the class instructor. Discuss your background with the Restaurant or in the restaurant industry.

Employees at the Restaurant

Identify the following leaders in the Restaurant Organization. Explain their role in the success of the Restaurant (or provide an opportunity for them to introduce themselves).

- Restaurant owner
- Area supervisor
- General manager
- Restaurant chef
- Assistant manager
- Front of house manager
- Back of the house manager
- Lead cook
- First cook
- Shift leader
- Certified trainers

History of the Restaurant

Start off with the name of the business and who owns it and where the restaurant is located in (what state)? Describe the restaurant concept (Uniqueness).

The Restaurant has created success by:

Examples are:

- Using the highest quality chicken, shrimp, and beef for all dishes.
- Accepting only friendly service and high quality food.
- Focusing on quick serve and take out business.
- Focusing on guest satisfaction, team building, and product excellence to lead the industry.

What is The Restaurant?

The Restaurant concept has always focused on serving fresh, high quality food, cooked to order and served in a friendly, exciting, and clean environment. All products used or sold in our restaurants are ordered from the Company's centralized warehouse. This centralized distribution helps us control product quality and consistency.

Orientation
Orientation Topics and Information

Mission:
To Be Exceptional with the Essentials
- Guest excellence
- Great tasting food
- Sparkling clean restaurants
- Positive profit line

Our Vision: Be Extraordinary with the Essentials

Our Credo: WOW each guest, each and every time; no excuses, no exceptions!

What it takes:
- **Integrity**- Be honest; hold yourself accountable for your actions.
- **Zeal to serve**- Going beyond the basics, desire to help others.
- **Excellence**- an attitude or feeling to strive for perfection, to do the best.
- **Teamwork**- everyone working towards a common goal and mutual respect for everyone's abilities.
- **Truthful communication**- Be specific with information. Set clear expectations.

Did You Receive…? Ask if team members have received the following items. Be prepared to explain all items. Distribute any missing items.
- **Job description:** Describes employee responsibilities and requirements for each job.
- **Menu description:** Describes and lists ingredients for each menu item.
- **Employee handbook:** Outlines employee benefits/laws, responsibilities, and Company information.
- **Restaurant training material:** Includes handouts and training guides.
- **Training agenda:** Schedules and training topics.

Breaks/Conditions/Teens:
Employers are responsible for providing employees with periodic breaks in a cool area, with fans or air conditioning, ventilation and cold beverages. The potential for heat stress is heightened for kitchen workers due to steam, hot grills and stoves.

Restaurant employees should be educated on the dangers and symptoms of heat stress, such as dehydration, exhaustion, fainting and heat stroke. Teenagers employed in the restaurant are only permitted to work limited hours until the age of 18. Children under 16 years of age are banned from baking or cooking, and using devices that may cause injury, such as stoves, knives and grills. Refer to your state for information regarding breaks and conditions.

Minor Breaks
Teen workers (under age 18) are entitled to an uninterrupted meal break of at least 30 minutes if they work more than 5 hours in a day. They also are entitled to at least a 10-minute paid rest break for each 4 hours worked. They must be allowed a rest period no later than the end of the third hour of the shift.

Regulations Breaks

Every employee is permitted (as far as practical) a rest period during each work period. The authorized rest period is based on the total hours worked daily. For every four hours of work time, every employee is allotted one ten-minute rest time. (Example, 2 breaks in an 8-hour shift, 1 break in a 4-hour shift) Team members who work less than 3.5 hours are not allotted a rest period.

Meals

- Team members who work more than 6 hours during a shift receive a minimum of 30 minute mealtime without pay.
- Team members who work less than 6 hours during a shift are not entitled to a 30-minute mealtime and can eat before or after signing in or during the allotted 10-minute rest period.
- Team members are eligible to enjoy items from the employee menu during each work shift.
- Team members can eat on schedule breaks or order takeout before clocking out.
- 6 hours or less entitled to a lunch employee meal (50% discount) excluding shrimp and white chicken dishes.
- 6 hours or more entitled to a lunch employee meal (free) excluding shrimp and white chicken dishes.

Conduct Off-Duty
Team members must adhere to the following guidelines when off duty:

- Team members are not permitted in the BOH or checkout areas.
- When entering the restaurant during business hours, team members must comply with the dress code and rules of conduct in front of our Guests.
- Team members must enter and leave through the front door only
- Team members are always welcome to enjoy our restaurant as a Guest. We simply ask that they comply with the standards of behavior and dress that we ask of our Guests. Also, the rules of conduct for on-duty team members apply to off-duty team members while on the premises. The employee's presence reflects on the restaurant and other team members who work for the Company.

Smoking

Smoking by team members is prohibited in the restaurant and food preparation areas. (Communicate the team members' designated smoking area at the restaurant). Remove all cigarette butts and debris from this area before returning to work from a "smoke-break." Note: Smokers do not receive extra breaks because they smoke.

Company Phone

Family members can call the restaurant main phone only in the event of an emergency. Employees are prohibited from using the restaurant house phone; this phone is reserved for restaurant business only. However, if you ask permission to use the phone the manager may be inclined to let you use the phone for local calls only.

Orientation
Orientation Topics and Information

Scheduling Postings

For example: Work schedules are posted by Thursday of each week. See your general manager for your restaurant's schedule posting.

Shift Switching

Permissible: only with authorization from the manager.

Overtime

Based on state laws overtime can be paid (time and a half) for every hour over 8 hours worked during a day or every hour over 40 hours worked during a week.

Calling Out

You are required to call at least 3 hours ahead of time if you know you are going to miss a shift. When possible, try to cover your own shift before making the phone call to your Manager.

Tardiness

Other team members, as well as your manager and our guests are depending on your prompt attendance to work. The restaurant does not tolerate tardiness. However, if you know you are going to be late, phone in and let the manager know as quickly as possible so arrangements can be made to cover that time. Continued tardiness can result in termination of employment from the restaurant.

Evaluation and Wages

Hiring wages are based on current experience in the restaurant industry. However, The restaurant recognizes excellent performance through increased salary.

Wage Increases

Over time, you can increase your earnings by demonstrating professionalism in the following areas:

- **Experience:** Starting wages depend on your experience in the restaurant industry.
- **Attitude:** A positive, "can-do" attitude with the desire to learn new skills and help team members accomplish the tasks required to complete a shift.
- **Consistent Performance:** Professional performance in your station, all team members are required to perform above standard.
- **Evaluation Ratings:** Evaluations provide a means of identifying areas of success and improvement for team members. All team members are provided the opportunity to complete an employee evaluation with their supervisor. Merit increases are reliant on above-average evaluations.

Evaluations:

Quarterly for Front of House Staff

FOH staff receives a quarterly evaluation to help identify areas of success and improvement. You should also conduct random audits of server performance, and review of the steps of service at any time, so that the servers remain consistent throughout the year.

Pay Periods

Checks are available on a regular basis depending on the payday policies. Be respectful of peak business hours when picking up paychecks. Best times 2-4 pm.

POS Time Keeping

Team members use the Point of Sale system to clock in and out. Conduct a training session for this procedure. Make sure team members know to immediately report any discrepancies in time to the Manager on Duty. Team members are charged for the replacement of lost or stolen cards, If applicable.

Pay and Benefits / Pay depends on experience

Remind all management and staff that they should not discuss their pay with another team member. That is private information designed for that employee based on experience, knowledge, education and training. Benefits will be explained by the General Manager on an individual basis.

At will employment

At will employment describes the employment relationship between employers and employees in almost every state.

At will employment means that the company does not offer tenured or guaranteed employment for any period of time to any employee without an employment contract or written direction from the CEO/President.

In at will employment either the company or the employee can terminate the employment relationship at any time, with or without cause, with or without notice.

Harassment

The Restaurant supports a no tolerance policy for harassment based on race, sex, religion, disabilities, or gender preference. No tolerance means the offender will automatically be investigated and possibly disciplined or terminated for any harassment allegations brought against him/her.

Parking

Most restaurants do not allow staff members to park in prime parking spaces. These areas are reserved for restaurant customers only. The owner of the restaurant will ultimately decide where staff members will park their vehicles while they are on duty. Make sure you park in a lighted area for safety. You can be fined for parking in handicapped spaces.

Orientation
Dress Codes

Dress Code, Uniform

The Restaurant requires every employee to wear a uniform (described below) while on the clock. As an employee of The Restaurant, you are our representative to the Guest. Uniforms help Guests easily identify team members who can help them. Uniforms are also designed for maximum safety while working.

The following uniform standards apply to every employee while:

- Working in the restaurant.
- Catering on location.
- Completing marketing assignments (delivering door hangers, etc.).

While wearing your uniform, especially when you are off the property or off the clock you are expected to act professional because you still represent the restaurant and the owner.

Grooming and Hygiene

Communicate the following grooming standards to team members:
- Hair clean and combed.
- Hair must be confined (a bun or up under a hat). If hair is in a ponytail and it hangs at shoulder length or longer, confine it further in a braid etc.)
- Hair color must be a natural color (not the color of the rainbow) unless the company specifies differently.
- Employees must be clean shaven. Goatees are allowed (If applicable) as long as they are kept neat and trimmed side's burns may not exceed mid-ear length. See management for facial hair guidelines.
- Fingernails trimmed and clean. Fake nails are not to be worn; nail polish will be neutral in color.
- Employees are expected to be clean, without excessive body odors or perfumes.
- Tattoos are to be covered up, by using Band-Aids or long sleeve shirts unless the company specifies differently.

Front of House Full/Part time

Name Tag (BOH). If applicable

Polo, short sleeve shirt, long sleeve shirt or a designed tee shirt (Depending on the season): If applicable

____ Polo's, shirts or tee shirts – shirt tucked into pants: If applicable

____ Hat or visor: If applicable

____ Apron: If applicable

Pants • Khaki or Black pants (no jeans or corduroys): If applicable

---

The following will be provided by the Employee.

See the hiring manager for work shoes purchase policy. If applicable

Oil/slip Resistant Shoes

Wal-Mart provides a special selection of non-slip shoes work and steel-toe shoes.

Orientation
Security

Safety is everyone's responsibility.

No one should ever open the back door at night. The reason for keeping the door closed is primarily for security reasons because of robberies.

In today's society, especially in today's economy, unfortunately robbery is a very common occurrence. You read about robberies in the newspaper, on the news and on TV. Businesses get robbed and people even get killed.

Most companies have very stiff policies about going out the back door at night; in fact, in a lot of companies they will terminate you if you have opened the back door at night, or if you prop the door open at any time. If a robbery occurs, it is important that you NEVER fight back. It only makes things worse. The safest thing to do is to cooperate and give them what they want. It is not worth putting yourself, your coworkers or customers lives in danger.

The best thing you can do is to be very observant

- How many people were involved?
- Could you tell if they were male or female?
- How tall was he/she?
- Hair color / eye color / skin color?
- What kind of clothes are being worn?
- Any visible marks on the robbers, such as – tattoos or cuts.
- Do any of the robbers have accents or speech impairments
- Did you see any vehicle when they arrived or left? Get the license number and the make/model, if possible.

Always enter the restaurant with two employees, at least one should be a manager, and usually the second is a cook or server. When the manager opens the door, a walk through needs to be conducted looking for anyone that might be hiding.

When closing the restaurant nightly, always lock the door for security reasons after the last customer leaves the restaurant.

When counting money never count in view of the guest, once the money is counted it need to be secured in a lock box or the safe in the office.

In some companies it is required for the employee to sign a policy/procedure agreement. This provides some sort of paper trail.

It is the owners and management's responsibility to promote a non-sexual harassment atmosphere. Managers or supervisors must not allow any type of sexual harassment to occur in the workplace. If sexual harassment occurs and the manager did nothing to fix it, then the manager is equally guilty and could be held accountable. If an employee files a lawsuit in regards to sexual harassment, then you are putting the restaurant in jeopardy. One single lawsuit will make a huge dent in your bottom line. Do you really want to take that chance?

What is Quid Pro Quo?

The Latin term quid pro quo translates to **"something for something."**

Therefore, quid pro quo harassment occurs in the workplace when a manager or other authority figure offers are merely hints that he or she will give the employee something (a raise or a promotion) in return for that employee satisfaction of a sexual demand. This also occurs when a manager or other authority figure says he or she will not fire or reprimand an employee in exchange for some type of sexual favor. A job applicant also may be the subject of this kind of harassment if the hiring decision was based on the acceptance or rejection of sexual advances.

For instance, a male bank manager interviewing a female applicant for a job as a teller places his hand on her thigh. When she objects, he asks, "Don't you want this job?" The implication is that she must comply with the hiring manager's advances in order to get hired.

Learn what sexual harassment is and how to prevent it in the workplace.

http://www.nolo.com/legal-encyclopedia/preventing-sexual-harassment-workplace-29851.html

It is unlawful to harass a person (an applicant or employee) because of that person's sex. Harassment can include "sexual harassment" or unwelcome sexual advances, requests for sexual favors, and other verbal or physical harassment of a sexual nature.

Harassment does not have to be of a sexual nature, however, and can include offensive remarks about a person's sex. For example, it is illegal to harass a woman by making offensive comments about women in general. Both victim and the harasser can be either a woman or a man, and the victim and harasser can be the same sex.

Although the law doesn't prohibit simple teasing, offhand comments, or isolated incidents that are not very serious, harassment is illegal when it is so frequent or severe that it creates a hostile or offensive work environment or when it results in an adverse employment decision (such as the victim being fired or demoted). The harasser can be the victim's supervisor, a supervisor in another area, a co-worker, or someone who is not an employee of the employer, such as a client or customer. Sexual harassment in the workplace can be very costly for the restaurant if you are in a lawsuit. Protect your assets and create a non-sexual harassment workplace.

Businesses that wish to foster an environment of cooperation and respect between the senior management team and employees creates open door policies. This policy leads to greater communication between managers and employees, but the policy must be monitored carefully to ensure the spirit in which it was created is not abused or compromised.

An open door policy allows employees to bypass their immediate supervisors and seek out senior managers to discuss job and personal issues. Much of the time, the issue is something the employee does not feel comfortable discussing with his immediate supervisor or his immediate supervisor is part of the issue.

With an open door policy, employees can approach senior management and discuss issues such as job performance, conflicts with co-workers, ideas for department improvements and company policies.

Open door policies foster communication between employees and management. The policy offers an alternative discussion forum for employees with supervisors who lack managerial skills or are prone to acts of intimidation.

The problem-solving skills of the management team also improve with such a policy; senior management encourages the employee to approach his immediate supervisor and also provides guidance to middle management for discovering managerial issues.

The policy creates an environment of trust between the employees and management. When an employee understands that he has someone to go to when his immediate supervisor is not an option, his trust in the company grows.

Open door policies can lead to employees automatically going over their immediate supervisor's heads for every issue. Bypassing immediate supervisors rob those supervisors of the ability to solve problems they normally would handle.

It also leads to tension between employees and middle management. Consistent bypassing might cause the manager to suspect the employee of undermining him in an attempt to cause problems between him and senior management.

Orientation
Open Door Policy

A business opting to institute an open door policy must be specific about rules put into place regarding its use. For example, an employee must attempt to discuss the issue with his immediate supervisor before involving a senior manager. It also must be clear that with the exception of obvious immediate supervisor malfeasance, the open door policy is not **a form of discipline for the immediate supervisor.**

The responsibility of ensuring that the proper channels are followed falls to senior management.

For example, if the issue is with that particular shift manager and the employee does not feel comfortable in discussing that issue with that manager, then the employee may use the open door policy chain of command. Make an appointment to speak to the general manager to voice your concerns. If the issue is still not resolved, then the next step is to go up the chain of command and speak to the owner or district manager.

If the problem still persists, keep moving up the chain of command until you are satisfied and the problem has been fixed. If you utilize the open door chain of command procedure, the employee should not be in fear of appraisal from any manager or other employee.

If this occurs, then immediately report that manager or staff member to the owner, general manager, district manager or human resources department. Remember the open door policy; follow the chain of command in order.

The minimum age for employment is 14 years old unless you are employed on a farm or domestic service, and then there are no restrictions.

Permits are required for all jobs except farm work:

- 12 years old to be a caddy at a golf course.
- You must be at least 11 years old to deliver newspapers.
- 7 years old for theater, modeling and television.
- No restrictions on the motion pictures.

Everyone less than 18 years of age needs an employment certificate (working papers) unless you are 17 and graduated or officially terminated from school.

There are three types of employment certificates in many states for Minors:

- General employment certificate: For any minor no longer enrolled in school.
- Vacation employment certificate: For any minor still enrolled in school.
- Transferable employment certitcate: For 16 or 17 year old minors. Can usually be transferred between employers. (Optional)

NOTE: Working papers are generally issued at the school where the child is enrolled.
Teenagers employed in the restaurant are only permitted to work limited hours until the age of 18. Children under 16 years of age are banned from baking or cooking, and using devices that may cause injury, such as stoves, knives and grills. Refer to your state for information regarding breaks and conditions.

Working papers are usually issued at the school where the child is enrolled.

Minor Breaks
Teen workers (under age 18) are entitled to an uninterrupted meal break of at least 30 minutes if they work more than 5 hours in a day. They also are entitled to at least a 10-minute paid rest break for each 4 hours worked. They must be allowed a rest period no later than the end of the third hour of the shift.

Orientation
Minor Laws

Overview of the minor hours of work (based on US regulations as of July 2016)
During the School year

14 and 15 year olds:

- Are not permitted to work more than **4 hours per day** and cannot work before 7 am or after 7 pm during the school year.

16 and 17 year olds:

- Not more than 8 hours per day and 28 hours per school week.
- Cannot work before 6 am or after 12 am (midnight) on school days before 6 am and 1 am on Fridays and Saturdays.

Summer time

During the summer time 14- 15 year olds are permitted a maximum of 8 hours per day and up to 10 pm.

There are no starting and stopping hour restrictions on what can be worked during the summer vacation, but at no time can a minor work more than 8 hours per day or 44 hours per week.

Penalties

There can be significant penalties for violating the Child Labor Law. Any person, including agents and managers, who violates the Child Labor Law can be sentenced to pay a fine for a first offense of between $200.00 and $400.00, and, on a subsequent offense, to pay a fine of between $750.00 and $1,500.00, or to undergo an imprisonment of not more than ten days, or both, at the discretion of the court.

The Pennsylvania Code also sets out specific penalties for violating individual Code sections, which can carry misdemeanor penalties. Refer to your state child laws for pertinent information regarding minors in your state.

In most cases the work permit is issued by the school where the child is attending. Instruct the minor to go to their school to obtain the application and then bring it back to the restaurant. The Manager or General Manager needs to fill out the form and then sign it.

Once the work permit is issued the minor needs to bring it back to the restaurant and a copy is made and that that copy is placed in the minor's employment file. The original work permit always stays with the minor.

You cannot let a minor work at any establishment without a validated work permit. Once again, please refer to your state laws as it is different from state to state.

Check your state, age requirements as it may be different from state to state

Check your state, age requirements as it may be different from state to state

Some prohibited occupations are:

- Bowling centers (except snack bar attendant, control desk clerk and scorer)
- Building heavy work
- Highway (open road)
- Where liquor is sold or dispensed
- Manufacturing
- Scaffolds and ladders
- Window cleaning (above ground)

These were just some examples of prohibited occupations under Pennsylvania's Child Labor Law. For more details on these and other occupations or any other information on the Child Labor Law, go online to http://www.dli.state.pa.us/ and click on Labor Laws or 1-800-932-0665

There may be additional restrictions placed on minors by the Federal Government.

You can find out more on their web site or by calling;
http://www.youthrules.dol.gov/Default.html
Call 1-866-4-USWAGE

Minor Laws are maybe different from state to state –

Please refer to your state laws so you can stay within the law.

Orientation
Occupational Safety and Health Administration (OSHA)

OSHA Training

The Restaurant is committed to a safe work environment and partners with the Occupational Safety and Health Administration (OSHA) to ensure each employee is trained and understands their responsibilities in maintaining a safe and healthy work environment. The OSHA Training provided by the restaurant outlines the practices for a safe environment.

OSHA Regulations for Restaurants

The United States Department of Labor Occupational Safety and Health Administration (OSHA) require that employers follow safety regulations to ensure the health of their employees.

Restaurant employees are protected under OSHA rules from poor conditions and hazards that may cause potential work-related injuries or fatalities. Establishments are inspected regularly to guarantee that employers are in compliance with OSHA guidelines.

Surface Maintenance

OSHA restaurant regulations include the maintenance of floors, aisles and walkways within all areas of the restaurant. OSHA law requires that passageways, storage rooms, kitchen areas, dining rooms, restrooms and bar areas are kept clean and dry.

Dishwashing stations or bar areas that are prone to water build-up should be provided with drainage, mats, false floors or platforms to prevent slipping or falling and related injuries. Floors must be free of protrusions, such as nails, and hazards, including loose boards, splinters and holes.

Aisles and passageways must be clear of obstructions and should be marked. Guardrails are required for stairs, steps, platforms and ramps.

Fire Safety

Restaurants need to supply portable fire extinguishers to protect employees in case of fire. Employers must inspect, maintain and test fire extinguishers. Maintenance is effective in ensuring the devices are fully charged and working.

Employers are required to provide a certification record signed and dated by the person who administered the fire extinguisher tests at the indicated time intervals required. Fire extinguishers should be stored in designated spots within the restaurant. Employers are responsible for alerting restaurant employees to where the fire extinguishers are located and informing them of a safety plan in place.

National Restaurant Association Educational Foundation
2055 L St. NW
Washington, DC 20036
Phone: 800.424.5156
Website: www.nraef.org

Pennsylvania Restaurant & Lodging Association
Their normal business hours are Monday through Friday, 8:30 AM. To 5:00 PM.
100 State Street
Harrisburg, PA 17101
Phone: (717) 232-4433 | (800) 345-5353
Fax: (717) 236-1202

Email: info@prla.org
Website: http://www.prla.org/

Certification Information
One certified food protection manager required per facility and accessible at all times during facility operation hours.

Serve Safe Certification Renewal Every 5 years.

New employees will have 90 days from starting employment to become certified. The online exam is now approved for use in the state. For additional information, contact PA Department of Agriculture.

All the above are Pennsylvania regulations – **Go to the National website to get more information on your state regulations:** http://www.nrfsp.com/en/State%20Regulations.aspx

Learn How to WOW Every Guest Every Time

24

Training Your Team

In this manual, we will be discussing training of the managers and other staff. This manual guides you through each training day. The training will consist of the training topics and materials of the day. The last part of each training day should consist of a discussion between the trainer and the trainee. There are also reviews and quizzes for each topic. To move forward each trainee needs to pass the quizzes and reviews, and the trainer should say they are ready to move to the next step. It would be pointless to let anyone move forward without absorbing the information. If poor training is given this causes confusion for the new person. If the current staff were poorly trained, then the confusion is even worse because the new person will get conflicting information. Whether you are just beginning your business, or you have been in business for a long time, it is important to have every employee trained properly. This means, if you have been in business, and you are not doing well and you identify problems with your employees, then step one should be "re-training" the current staff. Then you can hire on new staff to fill open positions. The more consistent you're training the better your chances of success.

The Training will be broken down and completed on a daily basis.

Day one should be an orientation for all new hires. I recommend that it is done in a large group. For instance, you just hired two cooks; three servers and one dishwasher complete their orientation together. Schedule a date and time that is convenient for the new hires' schedule and that is a time the trainer or a manager is free from other duties. Inform the new staff that it may take several hours to complete the orientation. Tell all new hires to bring with them a photo ID and a Social Security card, for the US, anyone under 18 must also bring in a work permit. Generally the work permit may be issued from the school guidance office. Minors should not be allowed to train or work until you have a valid copy of their work permit on file. Check your local area for laws on new hire paperwork.

It is recommended that the employees receive 14 or more days of training. However, we won't go through each area day by day. This manual is just an outline of how to train, not everything that an employee would need to know to complete their job. For example, we are not going to tell you how to cook different recipes. This would be important, but each restaurant has a unique menu, so we leave those details to you. You also know the layout of your restaurant, and the guests you serve. Ultimately, it will be up to you to decide how many days of training is needed and what the employee will be trained on a daily basis, but we strongly suggest you take the extra time at the beginning to get each employee off to a good start.

The initial investment may cost you more because you will be paying the trainer and the trainee along with the other staff working the restaurant. However, you need to think of this training time as an "investment" and not as an "expense." It will defiantly pay off in the long run as long as management and the staff do the right things for the right reasons according to how they were trained. The more you invest in proper training, the more likely your staff will stay with you, and be consistent in their work. This leads to greater profits and better employee morale. The advice given in this manual will ultimately help the employee and your business to be successful.

Servers must have great communication and interpersonal skills. They set the tone for the dining experience. Servers are actually sales staff for your restaurant, the sell your menu to the customers. They help customer's make food and drink decisions by utilizing suggestive selling or up-selling techniques. It is imperative that all servers know the menu items, ingredients and preparation methods inside and out.

Use of Time and Motion

Servers are normally assigned sections or stations. Each server should look for ways to save time and energy when serving your customers. All servers need to know how to be well organized and how to set priorities. For example, avoid unnecessary trips to the kitchen to increase time management. Multitasking is another way to save time and energy, for example, when you are pouring water at one table look around in your section to see if water is needed. Remember when a glass is half full, you should automatically refill the glass with water. If you serve all you can drink soda you should fill that glass automatically when the glass is half full.

Other ways to save time and motion are:

- Pre-busing more than one table.
- Delivering food and drinks to more than one table.
- Resetting more than one table.

Teamwork

Another very effective way to save time and motion is to train your staff in teamwork. Tell your staff members that one of the conditions of employment is to demonstrate teamwork daily.

What does Teamwork mean in a restaurant?

- Working together as a group toward a common goal.
- Solving problems together.
- Teamwork is achieving desired results.
- Servers should help out of their sections when possible.

Greeting Customers

Every restaurant employee should be responsible in greeting customers. If you see a customer at the door and your hands are full, then you can acknowledge the guest by saying "we will be right with you" either you seat that customer or find some to seat that customer. Inform management that there are guests at the door that need greeted.

If you are an employee on break or just arriving or departing the restaurant you should greet the guest or find some to seat that customer. Inform management that there are guest at the door that need greeted. Please remember the guest cannot tell the difference between an employee that is on the clock or the one that is off the clock. All employees when they on the restaurant property should always be in full, clean uniform. Also keep your shirt tucked in; after all you do represent the company.

Server Training
Server Job Description & Responsibilities

Dress appropriately
*Males – See management for proper uniform policies. If shirts or polo's are allowed shirts or polo's must be tucked in and a belt will be worn, clean khaki or black pressed pants, black non-slip shoes.
*Females: See management for proper uniform policies. If shirts or polo's are allowed shirts or polo's must be tucked in and a belt will be worn, clean khaki or black pressed pants, black non-slip shoes.

Hygiene
*Males: Fingernails trimmed and clean, clean-shaven and hair combed. Tattoos are to be covered up, by using Band-Aids or long sleeve shirts. See management for facial hair guidelines.
*Females: Hair that touches the shoulders, needs properly restrained.
Tattoos are to be covered up, by using Band-Aids or long sleeve shirts.
Fake nails are not to be worn; nail polish will be neutral in color.

Behavior
Must be upbeat at all times; always smile when in contact with the customers.
Respect the customers and staff at all times. No profanity is permitted in the restaurant, especially in the kitchen. No drug or alcohol use.
Hair that touches the shoulders, needs properly restrained.
Tattoos are to be covered up, by using Band-Aids or long sleeve shirts.
Fake nails are not to be worn; nail polish will be neutral in color.

Basic Job Description:
➤ Arrive to work 5 minutes before the shift begins.
➤ For communication purposes see the manager prior to starting the shift, communicate with the manager for pertinent information about the shift
➤ The number one priority is greeting the guest as they enter and depart the restaurant, this is everyone's responsibility
➤ The server's main responsibility for the servers is to provide exceptional customer service to each guest no matter what.

Part of our **WOW** customer service is to open the door as the guest enters and departs the restaurant.

Proper greeting verbiage is the key to good customer service. Greet the guest with a sincerely warm and friendly smile, every time a guest enters our restaurant you will say the following; "Hi, Welcome to "your restaurants name", how many people are in your party today?" If there are children or infants that require a highchair or booster, always ask, "Would you like a high chair or a booster seat today?" Also, make sure to say hello to the children. Make sure to move chairs if someone is in a wheelchair

When the guest departs the restaurant, always say: "Thank you for visiting - Your restaurants name we hope to see you again soon".

If your hands full and you physically cannot seat the guest, then acknowledge the guest by saying, "Welcome to - your restaurant's name, someone will be with you shortly," as you are walking in the dining room look for someone who can greet that guest.

Server Training
Server Job Description and Responsibilities

The first impression of the guests is how the Host or Hostess greets them. This first impression is an important part of customer service. Your greeting sets the tone in the customer's mind of whether this restaurant values their guests.

Seating the Guest – (Immediate seating) everyone is responsible in seating the guest

When seating the guest always stay with-in an arm length of the guest. Walk at the guest pace. Remember that any guest that is disabled or uses a cane or walker that they should be seated up front so the guest does not have to walk far to be seated.

Always offer high chairs and booster seats to families if needed. Make sure that they are clean. High chairs and boosters should be cleaned after a guest leaves the table. The strap to the high chair and boosters should be buckled. This tells anyone that the high chair or boosters have been cleaned.

Menus

- ➤ Help gather up all menus. Clean and sanitize menus and store them in the appropriate area.
- ➤ Every time you are on the floor such as, after seating a table or helping out your fellow servers always collect menus.
- ➤ If it is not busy then you should help other server's bus & reset the tables. (Teamwork)
- ➤ Food running is everyone's responsibility. If you pass the food pick up window and see food waiting to be delivered, then you should deliver it.

Expediting food to the guest:
- ➤ Hot food hot & cold food cold
- ➤ Proper plate presentation
- ➤ Cross checks the cook's ticket with what is on the plate to ensure that there is nothing missing.
- ➤ Clean plate rims
- ➤ Use a plate delivery towel to handle entrée dishes to ensure your hands do not touch the customer's plate.
- ➤ Inform the server that you ran the food or offer to assist the server with food delivery.

In some restaurants, servers may have gotten the impression that no one else should deliver the food to the guests, but this is not our philosophy. In reality, there are times the server cannot deliver the food within the ticket standard times because they are too busy greeting the tables, running drinks or other food items, pre-bussing and resetting tables or cashing out the guests. We do not want food sitting in the window waiting to deliver to the guests.

During the peak times, management or food runner needs to be in the position of the expo.
All employees; management, supervisors, servers, greeters, cooks are responsible for food running.
Once the entrees touch the food window, deliver the food quickly.
Servers are working as a complete team, if everyone works together, the shift will run smoother and professional.

Silverware Rolling

Servers are responsible for rolling silverware during the shift and at the end of their shift. Servers are to roll a pre-determined amount of silverware at the end of their shift Servers are to show the rolled silverware to the manager before completing their shift.

Suggestive Selling

All servers should know how to suggestively sell the menu. You need to know the menu by memory along with the menu ingredients.

Waitstaff Training

A well-trained server can be your restaurant's best sales tool. Without the proper knowledge, however, most attempts at upselling will fall short. Set up pre-meal briefings for your waitstaff where you review any special dishes and identify high-profit items they should focus on selling to the customers. Give regular wine education seminars so servers will know which bottles to recommend with which meals. Adding a bottle of wine to a meal can really boost the check size. You should even consider sending key servers out for sommelier training.

Entice Rather Than Sell

Encourage your waitstaff to use a soft-sell technique that uses descriptive language when explaining dishes to customers. Instead of simply asking guests if they want wine with dinner, servers can say, "We have an excellent reserve merlot that has won several recent awards, and it will complement that steak nicely. Can I interest you in a bottle?" When executed properly, customers will feel as though they have just received high-quality customer service instead of a sales pitch.

Read the Customers

Learn to read customers' body language and adapt your suggestions accordingly. If one of your customers seems indecisive or hesitant when ordering, jump in describe your favorite menu items. Take group dynamics into account when reading customers. Every table of customers will have its own personality. Knowing what that is will also help you determine when to sell and when to listen. Most groups of diners have an "alpha buyer," or someone who takes charge in the ordering process. Determine who that is and direct most of your upselling toward him.

Make Assumptions

When you make suggestions to customers, assume they want what you're selling. When a customer orders a vodka and cranberry, for example, a simple "We carry several brands of vodka. Would you prefer Grey Goose or Ketel One?" will almost always elicit a brand choice, changing that sale from a low-profit well drink into a high-profit premium cocktail. As you are making suggestions, look the customer in the eye, smile and gently nod your head as if you know they will answer in the affirmative.

Suggest High-Profit Items

The most expensive menu items are not necessarily the ones that bring in the highest profits. Gain a clear understanding of what dishes are the profit drivers, and focus on those when making suggestions to customers. Brief your waitstaff on which items they should be pushing and at what meals so that there is no uncertainty.

Up-Selling Techniques

Upselling is a common strategy for restaurants to boost their profits. By training your staff in ways to sell more, you can help their tips and improve business. Upselling is more than sales; it requires perception, knowledge and discretion. At its best, upselling can look less like sales and more like customer service; effective techniques should be subtle enough to avoid annoying the customer or making them feel pestered.

Offer More-Expensive Items

A common restaurant upselling technique is to offer more-expensive items than the ones the customer originally ordered. This tactic is most effective when it is not obvious. Servers often use this technique without the customer knowing by offering two choices of liquor without noting that one is more expensive, for example. In order to push up the bill, servers should have knowledge of the profit margins and prices of each item on the menu.

Extras

Many restaurants rely on a simple strategy to sell more: offering extra items. A fast food restaurant might ask customers if they'd like a super-sized option or if they would like fries with their meal. A restaurant server will ask a diner if they'd like to start with an appetizer or try a special entree. In some restaurants, the extras are prescribed by management: the chef's special or a new item they want to push, for example.

Offer Specific Items

Instead of asking customers if they would like additional food or drinks, it is often more effective to be specific. Restaurants often employ the strategy of avoiding generalities that are easy for the diners to dismiss. Instead of asking if a customer wants dessert, for example, the server will ask if they want to try the chef's special dessert and provide a mouthwatering description. This is particularly effective when the server can see that the customers are wavering; the delicious details can convince them to go with their desires.

Make Suggestions

When a customer is deliberating on what to order or asks for recommendations, a restaurant server has the opportunity to upsell without seeming pushy or irritating. They might name one of the more-expensive dishes on the menu when asked for a suggestion or recommend that the customer try a beverage that will complement their dish. By making helpful suggestions, the customer feels taken care of rather than like a sales target.

Server Training
Server Job Description and Responsibilities

Demonstrate Enthusiasm

One of the most effective upselling techniques a server can use is to show enthusiasm about the foods they are pushing. When they can give details about the food and a description of their personal experience and preference, it can be more convincing than simply suggesting an expensive item. For this technique to work, the server should be genuine

Servers are to work the six server steps of service to ensure WOW Customer satisfaction. Please remember all **time frames** that need to be met.

Door Greet
Immediate proper door greeting

Server Greets
The guest within two minutes of being seated by the greeter

Server Mentions
All specials (be descriptive when explaining to the guest what they are)

Server Suggest
A specific appetizer, (be descriptive), write down drink orders from left to right.

The Server Delivers
Drinks within four minutes, and delivers the appetizer with-in seven minutes.

Server writes down the entrée orders from left to right to prevent food auctioning. Remember Upselling and Suggestive-selling (the Sullivan nod).

Server for (POS Systems) you have two minutes to enter the complete order into the POS system.

For restaurants that do not have a (POS System) the appetizer orders need written down on a single ply order pad designated for that purpose. That order pad will be located on top of the kitchen food-selling window. Once you have written down the appetizer on the pad, give it to the cooks to prepare. Keep in mind you still need to write down that appetizer on the main guest check pad along with the price.

- **Breakfast:** standard times to prepare from the time the order was taken to the time it needs delivered is 10 minutes or less

- **Lunch:** standard times to prepare from the time the order was taken to the time it needs delivered is 12 minutes or less.

Servers are working as a complete team, if everyone works together, the shift will run smoother and professional.

- **Dinner:** standard times to prepare from the time the order was taken to the time it needs, delivered is 15 minutes or less, unless that particular food item needs additional time to prepare it. Please advise the guest it might take longer then normal to prepare the food.
- **Check back:** within two minutes or two bites, check back to the guest to ensure the meal is okay. Remember to pre-bus and do refills all throughout the meal period. In addition, if you are outside your assigned table section and pre-busing needs down, please make it happen (teamwork).
- **Dessert:** always bring to the guest on a large server tray all the desserts for the guest to view. The visual will sell better than verbal. The standard time to deliver the desert once it was written down is seven minutes. Up-sell by adding coffee or milk.
- **Check back:** within two minutes or two bites, check back to the guest to ensure the dessert is okay. Remember to pre-bus and do refills all throughout the meal period. In addition, if you are outside your assigned table section and pre-busing needs down, please make it happen (teamwork).
- For restaurants, without a (**POS System**) make sure you add the prices to the right of the check as you go.
- Once you determine if the guest orders dessert, then tally up the check, adding your states sales tax. The guest receives the original check in a guest check presenter standing up.
- When dropping off the check, include a carryout menu
- Receive payments and process credit cards and close the check out immediately
- Thank the guest with a warm, sincere smile and invite them back
- Immediately after the guest leaves clean the table per standards
- Wipe chairs, booths, high chairs and booster seats and clean floors
- Fill any condiments, as needed, including napkins
- Reset the table before the next seating

Server Training
Server Job Description and Responsibilities

Please remember to continually keep up with your server side.

Silverware responsibility is to continually roll silverware all throughout the shift and at the end of the shift, you must roll a designated amount of silverware and the Manager on duty must verify it.

Your table section must be cleaned, restocked and verified by management before you are done with your shift.

Must demonstrate team work 100%

Everyone is responsible in greeting the door and running food to guest.

Use of cell phones while working is prohibited including texting.

Every time you are in the dish room, (full hands in & full hands out)

These are very basic rules and job descriptions & responsibilities that occur in most restaurants everywhere.

Employee Name	Manager Name	Date

By signing this form you acknowledge that you fully read and understand the contents in this job description.

Suggestive Selling

All servers should know how to suggestively sell the menu. You need to know the menu by memory along with the menu ingredients.

Waitstaff Training

A well-trained server can be your restaurant's best sales tool. Without the proper knowledge, however, most attempts at upselling will fall short. Set up pre-meal briefings for your waitstaff where you review any special dishes and identify high-profit items they should focus on selling to the customers. Give regular wine education seminars so servers will know which bottles to recommend with which meals. Adding a bottle of wine to a meal can really boost the check size. You should even consider sending key servers out for sommelier training.

Entice Rather Than Sell

Encourage your waitstaff to use a soft-sell technique that uses descriptive language when explaining the menu to customers. Instead of simply asking guests if they want wine with dinner, the servers can say, "We have an excellent reserve Merlot that has won several recent awards, and it will complement that steak nicely. Can I interest you in a bottle?" When executed properly, customers will feel as though they have just received high-quality customer service instead of a sales pitch.

Read the Customers

Learn to read customers' body language and adapt your suggestions accordingly. If one of your customers seems indecisive or hesitant when ordering, jump in describing your favorite menu items. Take group dynamics into account when reading customers. Every table of customers will have its own personality. Knowing what that is will also help you determine when to sell and when to listen. Most groups of diners have an "alpha buyer," or someone who takes charge in the ordering process. Determine who that is and direct most of your upselling toward him.

Make Assumptions

When you make suggestions to customers, assume they want what you're selling. When a customer orders a vodka and cranberry, for example, a simple "We carry several brands of vodka. Would you prefer Grey Goose or Ketel One?" will almost always elicit a brand choice, changing that sale from a low-profit well drink into a high-profit premium cocktail. As you are making suggestions, look the customer in the eye, smile and gently nod your head as if you know they will answer in the affirmative.

Suggest High-Profit Items

The most expensive menu items are not necessarily the ones that bring in the highest profits. Gain a clear understanding of what dishes are the profit drivers, and focus on those when making suggestions to customers. Brief your wait staff on which items they should be pushing and at what meals so that there is no uncertainty.

Up-Selling Techniques

Upselling is a common strategy for restaurants to boost their profits. By training your staff in ways to sell more, you can help their tips and improve business. Upselling is more than sales; it requires perception, knowledge and discretion. At its best, upselling can look less like sales and more like customer service; effective techniques should be subtle enough to avoid annoying the customer or making them feel pestered.

Offer More-Expensive Items

A common restaurant upselling technique is to offer more-expensive items than the ones the customer originally ordered. This tactic is most effective when it is not obvious. Servers often use this technique without the customer knowing by offering two choices of liquor without noting that one is more expensive, for example. In order to push up the bill, servers should have knowledge of the profit margins and prices of each item on the menu.

Extras

Many restaurants rely on a simple strategy to sell more: offering extra items. A fast food restaurant might ask customers if they'd like a super-sized option or if they would like fries with their meal. A restaurant server will ask a diner if they'd like to start with an appetizer or try a special entree. In some restaurants, the extras are prescribed by management: the chef's special or a new item they want to push, for example.

Offer Specific Items

Instead of asking customers if they would like additional food or drinks, it is often more effective to be specific. Restaurants often employ the strategy of avoiding generalities that are easy for the diners to dismiss. Instead of asking if a customer wants dessert, for example, the server will ask if they want to try the chef's special dessert and provide a mouthwatering description. This is particularly effective when the server can see that the customers are wavering; the delicious details can convince them to go with their desires.

Make Suggestions

When a customer is deliberating on what to order or asks for recommendations, a restaurant server has the opportunity to upsell without seeming pushy or irritating. They might name one of the more-expensive dishes on the menu when asked for a suggestion or recommend that the customer try a beverage that will complement their dish. By making helpful suggestions, the customer feels taken care of rather than like a sales target.

Demonstrate Enthusiasm

One of the most effective upselling techniques a server can use is to show enthusiasm about the foods they are pushing. When they can give details about the food and a description of their personal experience and preference, it can be more convincing than simply suggesting an expensive item. For this technique to work, the server should be genuine

Greeter Position
The new server employee needs to be thoroughly coached in the server position.

Areas to touch on are: the greeter position, menu knowledge, POS training, server position, expeditor and food runner position.

The employee should master the greeter position. This employee needs to know: how to greet the guest with a warm, sincere smile. Learn the seating chart and how to seat the guest and where to seat the guest. Learn the greeter and server job description is the best way to jump start the training process.

Menu Knowledge
Learn the menu by memory; know the menu and the menu description. If a guest were to ask about a specific food allergy or the ingredients of a certain food product would you be able to answer the guest question without hesitation?

Point of Sale (POS) Training
The training server can practice entering factious food and drink items into the POS system. Each POS register should be able to activate the training mode in order for the new server to practice entering in the factious orders. The new server should be able to maneuver within the system to get familiar where all food and drink menu items are located on the POS desktop screen.

Server Training
Every manager, server and greeter should understand the WOW server steps of service. The server steps of service are how we greet, serve and treat each guest every time. It starts from the very minute they enter your restaurant until the pay their check and depart the restaurant. The server steps of service were designed to reduce or eliminate possible guest service issues. By following each step of service correctly and consistently the customers stay at your restaurant will not be jeopardized. In fact, if done right your customers may spread the positive word of mouth.

If you provide terrible service to your customers they may spread negative word of mouth to their family, friends and coworkers. Do not take that chance, establish a server steps of service training program now.

All servers including management and greeters should memorize the steps of service.
Go to: http://www.workplacewizards.com/steps-of-service/

Server Training
Six Steps of Service

Step 1

- Greet the Guest - Immediately upon the guest entering the Restaurant.
- Have a sincere, friendly smile.
- Hi, Welcome to "Your restaurant's name" how many in your party.

Step 2

- Seat the Guest – **Immediately** when there is an **open table**.
- Stay within arm's length of the guest as you are seating them.
- Senior Citizens – guest with walkers & canes **seat up front** if possible.
- Tell servers how many guest & what table number.

Step 3

- The server greets the table with a **sincere smile** within **2-Minutes**.
- The server places silverware on the table so other employees know they were greeted by the server.
- The server introduces herself by saying her **first name**.
- If you don't recognize the guest ask them if they have been here before.
- Talk about the **features** and **specials.**
- Start with the drink orders & suggestively sell an appetizer.

Step 4

- The server places the drink orders and appetizers in the POS system.
- Drink Orders are delivered within **4 Minutes** to the guest.
- The server takes the guest order from left to right.
- Enter the entire order into the **(POS)** system within **2 Minutes**.

Step 5

- Entrées are delivered to the guest within **15 Minutes.**
- Check back after **2 bites** to ensure everything is okay.
- Automatic refills and remove any dirty dishes.

Step 6

- Suggest desserts within **2 bites** of the guest finishing the entrees.
- Deliver the desserts within **7 Minutes** or less / suggest coffee or milk.
- Drop the check off (If server Banking) remind the guest that you will take the payment when they are ready.
- When receiving credit card payments, process and **close** the check out immediately, otherwise if you don't your table turn times will be affected.
- **Please thank** the guest with a warm, sincere smile and **invite them back**
- Reset the tables **immediately** after the guest leaves.
- Reset the table per standard and **wipe the seats** / **booths and clean floors** before the next seating.

Server Training
Six Steps of Service

On this page I will explain the entire step by step process of the server steps of service. The server steps of service if executed consistently and properly will yield excellent results.

Step 1

Greet the Guest immediately upon the guest entering the Restaurant. This step is the most important step in the entire process. Greeting the guest immediately will create the first impression. This is vital to repeat business. If you fail to create the first impression, then in the guest's mind they are thinking that the entire service may be below standard.

Invest in having a greeter on during peak time hours to ensure that your entire guests are properly greeted immediately and with a warm and friendly smile 100% of the time. I have seen successful restaurants where the owner/manager personally greets each guest as they walk through the front doors. Again in the customer's mind they are thinking WOW the owner/manager greeted us, this shows genuine concern in creating WOW customer service.

Having a sincere, friendly smile will have a huge impact on what your customers think about your restaurant and service.

Hi, Welcome to "your restaurant's name" how many in your party. You are welcoming your guest to the restaurant by mentioning your restaurant's name and at the same time you are saving steps by asking how many are in your party. During this process you should have the correct amount of menus ready based on the group amount.

Step 2

Seat the Guest immediately. Customers may get upset if they see open tables and they are not seated.

If you have an open table because they are reserved, then it might be a great idea to place a reserved table tent card on that table so that guest and staff members see that that particular table is reserved.

If for some reason a server cannot wait on that customer, and then find another server that can wait on that table. Do not let the customer wait as this will create a negative experience. Stay within arm's length of the guest. You are leading them to the table; make sure that you are walking the same pace as your customers are. Senior Citizens. Guest with walkers & cane's seat up front if possible. Always be considerate to the elderly and their needs. Quote them a reasonable time to be seated.

Tell servers how many guest & what table number. After seating the customers at that table, the assigned server should be notified that they were seated in their section and how many are in the group. Some restaurants utilize greeters or other employees to greet the table and help out with the drink order until the assigned server can approach them.

Step 3

The server should greet the table with a warm and sincere smile within 2-minutes. Customers expect prompt service at a reasonable time frame. If the assigned server cannot get to the table within the 2 minute time frame, then find another server who can. Make sure the manager on duty is advised so they can approach the table and do what they must do to fix the issue.

The server places silverware on the table so other employees know they were greeted by the server.

Placing the silverware on the tables as the guest are seated serves 2 purposes. If there are customers seated at any particular table with no silverware, then the server has not approached them.

There are times that customer's entrées are delivered to the tables with no silverware in sight. The customer flags down another employee to tell them that the table is in need of silverware. That tells the customer that the restaurant is unorganized. To prevent this from happening always have silverware at the table as the guest are being seated.

Server introduces his or herself by saying their first name. Be personable and professional during the first initial greeting. Always introduce yourself to your customers by saying your first name.

If you don't recognize the guest ask them if they have been here before. If this is the very first time that that customer visited the restaurant, then treat them as they are a very important person (VIP). Inform management and staff members as well. Customers love attention. This is the restaurants opportunity to impress the customer. When placing the order with the cooks also inform them of the VIP. Creating great customer service with VIPS will create repeat business. Don't get me wrong all guests should be treated as if they are VIP's. Train your staff to treat each guest as if they were a popular movie star. With that mentality your restaurant will go far.

Talk about the features and specials. This is an excellent to time suggest and upsell the menu. After all, restaurants are in the business of making money. If the server upsells the menu that means more money on the customers check. As long as the server provides WOW service, then the customer will leave a larger tip and the restaurant will generate more revenue.

Start with the drink orders & suggestively sell an appetizer. Start off by taking a drink order from left to right. Write down the drink order onto the server pad from top to bottom. When the drinks are delivered to the table, you will know who gets what drink.

Before approaching the customers table profile the table by determining what the guest may order based on the age group and the table size. Always have a specific appetizer in mind as you approach the table. Never ask the guest "Would you like to order an appetizer? Always be descriptive when describing the appetizer.

Step 3

Cheese Sticks Appetizer

Would you like to try our cheese stick appetizer, fried to a golden brown texture with melted gooey mozzarella cheese inside served with our very own marinara sauce? If you are describing the appetizers to the customer, you have a greater chance of selling that particular appetizer.

In return you will generate more income for you and the restaurant. If the table is a large group, then you may want to upsell an appetizer such as a sampler platter or a combo appetizer. If the tables are senior citizens, then a light appetizer may be appropriate or a non-spicy appetizer.

If the table has children, then try selling mozzarella sticks or chicken tender appetizers. This might be a great opportunity to sell 2 appetizers to a table. Try selling 2 appetizers to large groups. If the table has adults and children, then sell the kid's mozzarella sticks or chicken tender appetizers and then sell the adults a different appetizer.

Step 4

The server enters the drink order, soup, salad or appetizers in the POS system within the standard check time. After taking the drink, soup, salad orders or appetizers from the customers, immediately enter that information into the POS system.

I have seen servers by passing entering the drink, soup or salad orders into the POS system because they believe that it will put them behind. They also claim they have a great memory, saying that they will not forget to place that order into the POS system at a later time.

This is not so, these servers may forget to place these orders into the POS system creating a loss in revenue. After all, they are only human, they will make mistakes. This is why systems are put into place to ensure minimal mistakes.

It will literally take **1 minute or less** to place the drink, soup, and salad or appetizer order into the POS system. You have **4 minutes** from the time the order was placed to deliver the drinks, soup or salad to the guest. The appetizer should be delivered to the guest within **7 minutes** from the time you placed the order into the POS system.

Drink Orders are delivered within **4 Minutes** to the guest.

The server takes the guest food order from **left to right**. It is very important that servers use server check pads to write down the customer's orders from left to right.

Enter the entire order into the **(POS)** system within **2 Minutes**.

Step 5

Breakfast should be delivered to the guest within 10 minutes or less. Lunch should be delivered to the guest in **12 minutes or less** and dinner should be delivered to the guest in **15 minutes or less**. In most restaurants customers will expect their food quickly.

In upscale restaurants it may take longer to serve customers mainly because most of the food is made from scratch and some of the menu items may be more complicated due to the ingredients. Steaks may take longer to prepare because the guest may want a medium well or a well done steak. In this case tell the guest it may take a bit longer to prepare the steak.

If for some reason the check times are falling behind in the kitchen, inform management, and then tell your guest it may take a bit longer to receive their food. Do not wait until your guest flags you down to ask you where the food is, be honest.

Customers will understand honesty. Managers should help the kitchen when they fall behind to bad customer service. Be proactive before issues occur.

Step 5

Check back after **2 bites** to ensure everything is okay. This step is very important. It will tell you if the guest is dissatisfied. Look for body language like rolling eyes, arms crossed or an upset face expression. Maybe the guest has not touched their food.

Whatever the issue is correct, the problem. You may have to remake the food or take the food off of the check depending on the severity of the problem. Always inform management of any customer complaints.

Automatic refills and remove any **dirty dishes**.   Do you want to really **WOW your customers?** Do drink refills automatically when their glass is half full; do not wait for the customer to flag you down.

Educate the entire front of the house staff to help out outside of their sections and do drink **refills** and **pre-bussing (teamwork).**

Step 6

Suggest desserts within **2 bites** of the guest finishing the entrees. Some restaurants have a demo dessert tray set up prior to selling desserts to their customers. By using a demo dessert tray the customer can actually see what the dessert looks like and there is a greater chance of selling that dessert to the guest. You can also plant the idea in the customers mind just before they are done with their entrée by saying" leave room for dessert.

When approaching your guest, have a certain dessert in mind and sell it to them by describing it. You need to develop a sales person mentality and upsell the menu or suggestively sell the menu. Practice on your days off, learn selling techniques on how to approach the guest and successfully sell the menu. Stand in front of a mirror or in front of another person and perfect it. Remember, you do not want to be robotic in nature. It needs to be short and natural. For example, describing chocolate cake; would you like to try our chocolate cake, it is very moist and flavorful in every bite. It is simply delicious.

Deliver the desserts within **7 Minutes or less** / suggest coffee or milk.

Drop the check off (If server Banking) remind the guest that you will take the payment when they are ready. If you do not have server banking, then print the check off at the front register and drop it off **immediately**.

Step 6

On the back of the check write thank you and print your name on it. This also might be a great time to upsell carry out desserts, if the guest did not order a dessert, simply ask them if they would like to add a carryout dessert to the check to take home. When presenting the guest check, use a check presenter; place the check in it along with a pen.

Remember to stand the presenter upward when placing it on the table. Customers hate being pestered when it is time to cash them out. If you see the presenter lying down directly on the table, then most likely the payment is ready to be processed. If you use American express you might be able to order check presenters for free. Contact them directly or contact your credit card processing representative. When receiving credit card payments, process and close the check out immediately, otherwise if you don't your table turn times will be affected. Please thank the guest with a warm, sincere smile and invite them back. Reset the tables immediately after the guest leaves.

Reset the table **per standard and wipe the seats / booths** and clean **floors** before the next seating. The quicker you can turn your tables the more revenue you and the restaurant can make. **Pre-bussing** your tables will also help in this process. Hiring bussers may be a bit more costly, although in the long run, the more seating you have them more revenue you produce.

If for some reason the servers cannot reset the tables quickly, then you will have a dining room full of dirty un-bussed tables.

What if you have a wait up front and those guests see all those empty un-bussed tables? Two things may happen:

- The guest may stay, but the **first impression was blown**. You can forget about repeat business unless you can successfully recover the guest experience.
- The guest will leave and **visit your competition**. Again, you can forget about repeat business.

Greeting Customers

Management should train all employees in customer greeting procedures and seating procedures. Employees in the back of the house also are responsible in greeting customers. Kitchen staff must remove their apron before they are in the presence of customers.

Train your management and staff members in doing the right thing for the right reasons. Managers/Owners set the tone for excellence in the workplace.

Help deliver food and drinks

Demonstrate Teamwork by helping your co-workers you the (server) in delivering food and drinks. Make sure you inform that particular server that you ran or delivered their food or drinks to that customer. If everyone was motivated in demonstrating teamwork throughout the entire shift, your restaurant will run more efficient and repeat business will produce higher profits for both the server and restaurant.

There is no "I" in a team, it is "**we**". Servers should never tell other servers not to run their food or drinks. Most restaurants today utilize teamwork in their restaurant. Server's tips and the restaurant revenue will be affected if the server tells another server not to run their food, especially if that server falls behind and is unable to run their food on time.

That is why there are expeditors, food runners and other servers who demonstrate teamwork and create the **WOW effect.** A great idea is to post near the food window the server dining room chart that shows the server sections and table numbers. This will benefit the servers in making sure the food is delivered to the correct table. Before running the food to the customers, match up what is on the plate to the customer's ticket to ensure nothing is missing. Hot food hot and cold food cold. If you do not see steam coming off the food, tell the cooks to reheat it. You do not want to serve cold food to any customer; this will create complaints that will affect your tip and restaurant's revenue. Be proactive and correct the issue before it becomes a problem.

Pre-busing (Sharking Tables)

Sharking is when you walk through the dining room pre-busing tables: always pre-bus your tables and if possible help pre-bus out of your section. **For example**, if you are entering another servers section and there are plates that can be pre-bussed do it. You will be creating the WOW effect.

Hopefully that server in that section will help you out in that section. If everyone had that mentality, then the shift will run smoother. If another server helps you out by delivering food or pre-bussing your section, that is a good thing, it creates teamwork and excellent customer service
Imagine this, if everyone demonstrated teamwork 100% of the time, then repeat business will be ongoing which equals consistent revenue for all employees and the restaurant. The more people you **Wow** the more revenue have generated as long as you do the right things for the right reasons.

In most states the server pay is below $3.00 mainly because they receive tips. If the server does not bring in an average (minimum wage) for 1 hours work from their tips, then the server must be paid minimum wage or more.

In most cases you can afford more than one server on the floor at any given time and it is recommended that each server be assigned 4 to 5 tables per section, this will assure that the guest will be properly taken care of.

Allowing the servers to have more tables than they can handle can create a negative guest experience. Let me explain, the server has a lot of tasks that need to be done in a short period of time, for example: Liz has a full section and two of the tables have been serviced and table # 3 received the drinks, although they are now waiting to place their orders and Liz has not greeted the 4th table, in the meantime one of the first 2 tables flagged her down because there is hair in their food and it's not getting any better because the hostess sat her a 5th table.

Assigning 2 servers per section is a great idea, this way the servers can handle more tables with better service because both servers can help each other out taking orders, delivering food and drinks and pre-busing tables.

There are servers who can multitask their way out of this nightmare and there are servers who will break under pressure and in return you will lose that guest which equals less profits.

There will be times that the manager on duty will have to help the servers with drink refills, delivering food to the guests, taking food orders and entering the food orders into the POS system.

The guest expects WOW service and they also expect to receive both service and food in a timely manner.

The servers steps of service if properly executed consistently will ensure that each guest receives top notch service.

Owners, management and staff members should know the server steps of service by memory. Management should ensure that the steps of service are done consistently and correctly on every shift. If management observes a particular server not demonstrating the steps of service, then that server should be re-trained or moved into a different position. Letting a server remain in the serving position without demonstrating the steps may create a negative domino effect.

If management does not follow through on all policies and procedures, including the steps of service, your restaurant employees will run the restaurant down to the ground fast. Management may not be respected by the staff members and repeat business will decrease dramatically.

Is this what you want? Make sure this does not happen to your restaurant.

Server Training
Server Position Training

It would be a really good idea to train a lead server or training server and management prior to training the remainder of the staff. The lead server or training server responsibility will be to train your serving staff. Normally the training server will make more money per hour and may receive free meals only when she or he trains. This will help boost the trainer's work ethic and moral.

Make sure you utilize the trainer as a second pair of eyes to help pinpoint areas of opportunity while they are working normal shifts. Give your trainer authority to correct all staff members in customer service and the steps of service during all shifts. Make your staff aware that the trainer will be in a supervisory capacity during all shifts. Make it a habit to inform new hires during the orientation process.

While your trainers are working normal shifts for, example, servers are to be paid server rate of pay. Still allow them to be your second pair eyes.

Train your server trainers to be respectful and professional when dealing with staff members. Inform the trainers to always correct employees away from other employees and customers to avoid embarrassment.

Trainers should at times ask management on how to deal with employees in certain situations. Making a server trainer as a supervisor is definitely an investment with returns.

The new hire will train with a server trainer per your scheduled training time.

Explain to the trainee what is expected from them during and after the training process. Be detailed as this will help clarify the process. The new hire will know what is expected from them.

You can use a server training sign off sheet to keep track of the entire training process. As you train the server in different areas of the server position you can sign them off showing that they were certified in that area.

Silverware Rolling
Servers are responsible for rolling silverware during the shift and at the end of their shift. Servers are to roll a pre-determined amount of silverware at the end of their shift Servers are to show the rolled silverware to the manager before completing their shift.

http://www.workplacewizards.com/restaurant-server-training-checklist/

Server Training
How to Roll Silverware into a Paper Napkin

Step 1

Fold the napkin into a smaller square, if needed. This largely depends on the type of napkin you use. Paper napkins come folded in the package, but cloth napkins, usually require folding them twice. The diagonal measurement of the napkin from corner to corner should be at least 2 inches longer than the knife, but rolling is easiest when the knife length is about two-thirds this length.

Step 2

Lay the napkin on the table in front of you. Turn the square so it's a diamond with one corner pointing toward you.

Step 3

Lay the knife horizontally in the center of the diamond with the tip of the blade 1 inch from the left corner. If you use small paper napkins the knife might extend beyond the corner which leaves the tip exposed.

Step 4

Place the fork on top of the knife so the bottom of the fork is even with the bottom of the knife. Place the spoon on top of the fork, nestled in the fork's curve.

Step 5

Fold the bottom corner -- the corner pointing toward your body -- up to cover the silverware handles. Hold the napkin tight against the sides of the silverware. The tip of the corner that you fold falls in perfect line with the top corner of the napkin, but falls short of perfectly overlapping the top corner.

Step 6

Fold in the right-hand corner of the napkin so the napkin is tight against the bottom of the knife. Line up the fold to the side of the silverware that faces you. Keep everything as tight as possible.

Step 7

Fold in the left-hand corner to cover the ends of the silverware, if possible. This depends on the napkin size.

Step 8

Roll the silverware away from your body toward the top corner of the napkin. While you might need to use both hands and roll slowly to keep everything tight, with enough practice, you can roll the silverware quickly with just the palm of your hand. Hold the fold at the bottom of the silverware with your right hand, place your palm on top of the silverware and simply push your hand away from your body to roll a napkin quickly.

Step 9

Tuck the top corner of the napkin under the silverware to keep it from unrolling. Slip a napkin ring over the rolled silverware and napkin, if desired, particularly if the top corner of the napkin doesn't end perfectly under the stacked silverware. Restaurants commonly wrap rolled silverware with a paper strip that has adhesive to stick it to itself, much like the adhesive side of a sticky notepad.

Silverware & Plate Placement
Table Setting

THE INFORMAL TABLE SETTING

At an informal meal, all flatware is laid on the table at one time. At the host's option the dessert utensils may be brought to the table on the dessert plate.

The following is a standard table setting for a three-course meal. Note the basic "outside-in" rule. The piece of flatware that will be used last is placed directly next to the whatever plate you are using.

FORKS

Both forks are placed on the left of the plate. The fork furthest from the plate is for salad. The fork next to the plate is for the dinner. (Please Note: At more formal meals where the salad is served after the main course, the order of placement is reversed.)

Fork tines may be placed downward, in the continental style, or upward, in the American style.

DINNER PLATE

The dinner plate is placed on the table when the main course is served and is not on the table when the guests sit down.

Large plates, such as the dinner plate and luncheon plate, are laid about one (1) inch in from the edge of the table.

SALAD PLATE

The salad plate is placed to the left of the forks.

Small plates, such as the salad plate, fish plate, and dessert plate, are laid about two (2) inches in from the edge of the table.

DINNER KNIFE

The dinner knife is placed on the right side, and directly next to and one (1) inch away from, the plate. The blade should face the plate. If the main course requires a steak knife, it may be substituted for the dinner knife.

SPOONS

The soup spoon is on the far right of the outside knife.

THE PLAN

Try to plan the table setting to match your menu. When bread and butter are served, add a butter plate to the table. Use separate salad plates if serving your main course with gravy. Depending upon the occasion, you may want to use a "formal" table setting or an "informal" table setting. For most of us, the need to set a truly formal table is almost nonexistent.

TABLECLOTHS AND PLACE MATS (TABLE LINENS)

Although a formal dinner requires either a tablecloth, at informal dinners a tablecloth is optional. A bare table with place mats is the alternative.

DINNERWARE, FLATWARE, GLASSWARE

If you don't have enough good china and flatware to create place settings for your guests, you have three alternatives. The first is to visit your local party supply store. Most have an extensive collection of formal tableware for rent. The second is to create a second table setting at a smaller table with your everyday dinnerware, or use borrowed dishes and place settings. The third choice, for casual dinners, is to mix and match.

CENTERPIECES AND CANDLES

Flowers or bowls of fruit work well as a centerpiece. Make sure the centerpiece doesn't stand so tall that guests can't see over it. Candles, if meant to be merely ornamental, are placed on either side of the centerpiece. Or, place one candle above each place setting if they will be used as the only source of light.

WINE TASTING ETIQUETTE

Once it is poured into the proper glass, it's time to evaluate and enjoy the wine. Evaluating wine involves four basic steps – looking, swirling, smelling, and tasting.

Step 1

Look. Holding the wine glass up against a white background, such as a napkin or table cloth, to evaluate its color and clarity. Red wines should range in color from deep purple to brick red. White wines should range in color from lemon gold to golden amber.

Step 2

Swirl. Swirl the wine in your glass to aerate it.

Step 3

Smell. Put your nose in the glass and take a deep breath. Older wines should have subtler aromas than younger ones.

Step 4

Taste. To taste the wine, fill your mouth about ½ full and subtly swish the wine around.

Server Training
Techniques for Great Training

Shadowing

The new hire shadows the trainer for several hours during the slowest peak times normally, breakfast or lunch. Never train during heavy peak times, especially during the weekends. It is important that the new hire only observe the trainer serving the guest.

Once the trainer is comfortable that the new hire understands the process, then the trainer can shadow the new hire correcting them as they go. Never let a new hire wait on a table by themselves during this particular process.

Servers with experience and servers with no experience need to go through the same process. You need to validate that these servers know how to serve the customer per your standards and not theirs. Every restaurant has a base for serving, although each restaurant differs in style, policies and procedures.

You need to make absolutely sure that each server whether they have experience or not to know what you expect from them, otherwise the consistency will be off and believe me the guest will notice that.

Questions and Answers

During the training process the trainer should be asking plenty of questions to ensure that the new hire has retained the information by memory. If the new hire does not know the answer or hesitates to answer the question correctly, then the trainer should periodically ask that same question until the new hire actually answers the question correctly from memory. This is a very important step in the training process; never let a server or any employee excel to the next step without mastering the previous step.

Show, Do & Review
- **Show** the new hire how to correctly perform the task.
- Let the new hire **Do** the task correctly.
- **Review** with the new hire the task to ensure the information was retained by memory.

Role Playing

Choose a time during off peak times to train. This is a group training process. Sit the entire group away from other guest or utilize a training room. Choose several new hires and let them role play as a guest.

The trainers will role play as an actual server serving the training new hires as they role play as a customer. This is an excellent training opportunity for all new hires to actually watch the trainer on how to correctly approach the customer and how to serve the guest through the entire process. Each new hire will rotate role playing the customer and the server until the trainer feels comfortable in knowing that each new hire understands and demonstrates by memory this process.

Servers are to take the guest orders from left to right. As they take the customer's order from left to right, the server writes the order down onto a server pad from top to bottom. The first order belongs to the customer on the left and the last order belongs to the customer all the way to the right.

The point of doing this is as the food is delivered to the customer it goes to the correct customer without auctioning the food off, this looks very unprofessional to the customer if done in this particular manner.

If your restaurant does not have a POS system

Make sure all severs are using a carbon copy server pad. The original copy stays with the server and the copy goes to the kitchen. Use a check stabber for the kitchen check copy. The cook's will prepare the customer's food order from the copy. When the cooks complete the entire order and the food is in the window, the cook will place that check near that particular order. Do not place that guest check on top of the food. When the food is ready to be delivered to the customer the check will be stabbed onto the check saber.

At the end of each meal period the manager will collect all the checks from the kitchen check stabber and match them up against the guest checks located at the front registers. This keeps the servers honest. If you have a dishonest server, all they have to do is throw away the kitchens copy and pocket the cash. It is best to let a greeter or cashier ring out the customer and be responsible for that particular guest check.

If the server is ordering an appetizer, then write a separate check and give it to the kitchen for preparation. Verbally communicate to the cooks that this is a priority appetizer check. Do not forget to write down that particular appetizer on the main customer check.

Every manager, server and greeter should know how to manually write out guest checks in case the POS system goes down. Also have a manual credit card imprinter machine available with 2 part manual charge card slips. Your credit card merchant company can point you in the right direction for these types of supplies or go to: https://www.amazon.com/s/ref=nb_sb_noss_1/183-5876932-1090465?url=search-alias%3Doffice-products&field-keywords=credit+card+imprinters

All Kids meals should be prepared and delivered before the adult entrée's.

Let us say that the guest check made it up to the front and they were cashed out. You are now missing the kitchen copy of that particular check. If this is a consistent occurrence and it is the same server each time, then it is safe to say something is going on. You might even notice a food cost issue. Never confront that server until you have enough documentation to support that incident.

Collecting Documentation
- Start by collecting all the servers' kitchen / front register customers checks pertaining to each incident.
- Staple each set together.
- Document each incident on paper.

Remember to note that each day's incident only involves one particular server. Every other server on those particular days had no missing checks. What are the odds that it is only that one particular server? Never discuss with anyone except management your findings.

You could set up pin-hole cameras in several areas of your restaurant to record such activities.

To be proactive means is to head off issues before they become problems.

Set up permanent security cameras in areas such as:

- Near the front and back doors
- Server aisle & food pick up area
- Near all cash registers or (POS) systems
- Kitchen
- Manager's office
- Parking lot

You might be thinking that this will be costly. Think of it as an investment, your cash & alcohol shortages and food inventory will be at a minimal loss. It is a fact that 70% of your revenue losses are directly related to your employees. Not all of it is theft; improper training, server or cook mistakes, food, alcohol remakes, customer complaints, food, alcohol discounts or comps play a huge role in revenue loss.

It's your money, WHAT'S IN YOUR WALLET?

Master the steps of service 100% as this will definitely create WOW customer service

Soup, Side Salads, Appetizers and Soda's/Drinks

Normally the customers will order an appetizer and drinks before they decide what they want to order as their main dish. Go to the POS system directly after taking the appetizer and drink order.

Open up a check and make sure you open the correct table number, enter the appetizer order and fire it to the kitchen. It should take **7 minutes or less** to get that order to the guest. That check needs to be a priority check.

Drink orders should go out to the guest within **4 minutes or less** from the time the guest ordered it. Never bypass the POS, get in the habit of entering the information as you get it from the customer. If you bypass the POS you might forget to place that order into the POS later which will create loss revenue.

Server Training
The Food Bell System

The cooks may sell the entries by ringing a bell and saying not yelling, for example, "15 minute check" all employees must run that food to the guest. Any employee, a manager, server or cook in the area that heard the cook saying "15 minute check" should run the food to the customer. It would be a great idea to train all staff members on how to use the seating chart and where the tables are located by table numbers.

By expediting the food to the guest it creates good check times, hot quality food and less guest complaints. This is a good working system I know I have worked in several restaurants that use this system.

There are different systems that will help in food delivery to the customers.

Vibrating Server Pagers/ Electronic Food Pagers

The cooks or expeditor will press a button that is associated with a particular server; the pager will vibrate telling the server that food needs to be run to the guest.

Numbered Light Panel System

The cook will notify a server that food needs ran to the customer by pressing a button associated with a particular server, a numbered light will light up on the dining room numbered light panel system.

Full Time / Part Time Expeditor

This employee typically is located on the opposite end of the kitchen (server area). He / She will make sure that whatever is on the kitchens copy of the check is on the plate. They will check for hot food hot and cold food cold. Plate presentation: garnishes. The golden rule is when the kitchen sells a check; it is to be delivered to the guest within 20 seconds. This is to ensure that the food remains hot and fresh.

The expeditor will work with food runners delivering food and drinks to the guest as it is placed in the food windows by the cooks. Some restaurants do not have the luxury of having expeditors or food runners because of low sales or because they are a low volume store. In this case every staff member needs to help deliver food to the guest including management.

Standard Ticket Times

Breakfast	10 Minutes or less
Lunch	12 Minutes or less
Dinner	15 Minutes or less
Dessert	7 Minutes or less
Appetizers	7 Minutes or less
Soup/salad/soda	4 Minutes or less

There is no "<u>I</u>" in team, it's "WE".

Shifts will run more smoothly when teamwork exists. In most restaurant teamwork is required.

Everyone helps out everyone that is the mentality that you should have every time you are at the restaurant. Let us use this example: A Bicycle chain with links; if the links in the bicycle chain are not broken then when you peddle the bike it will take you places.

If the bicycle chain is broken it will not move and you may be stuck wherever it broke down. My point is if one person decides not to demonstrate teamwork during the shift the shift may fall apart because someone may have to pick up the slack and that puts everyone behind and they have to work harder.

Sense of Urgency

In the restaurant business you are expected to apply a sense of urgency all throughout your shift. As the restaurant gets busier, especially during peak times, everyone needs to pick up the pace so that the shift does not fall behind, especially when selling food in the kitchen. Just like teamwork when someone decides not to apply a sense of urgency then you put the shift in jeopardy. Each training, employee before being validated in each kitchen position needs to master the position. The manager will evaluate the employee at the end of each training day with questions and answers to ensure that the employee retained the information.

Clean As You Go Procedures

All employees new and old are required to clean as you go, before, during and at the end of every shift. At your assigned stations, you are to keep the area clean, sanitized and organized. Also have a sanitation bucket with clean sanitation water and a clean towel in it. There are no excuses for a dirty work station.

Before smoke breaks, lunch breaks or 15 minute breaks are given your station must be clean, sanitized, organized and stocked. All breaks must be approved by management. No breaks are given during any peak time period or if business is busier than normal.

When the checks are cleared from the rail, you need to clean, organized and stock your station. When you are done with cleaning, organizing and stocking your station see management for other cleaning assignments. Minors are the exception to the rule, they must have a break within a four hour period.

Server Training
Restaurant Certified Trainers

This is one of the most important positions to set the tone for the correct procedures that need to be installed in all employees.

In order for the training process to be effective the trainers need to be selected by the following criteria:

- Consistency in following all established policies and procedures.
- Mature in age and in doing the right thing.
- Takes criticism well and uses it toward correcting the issue.
- Respects all other employees, including the management team.
- Does not follow the crowd, but sticks to what is correct.
- Position knowledge and execution above standard.
- Has the best interest of the restaurant in mind.
- Has a passion for keeping the business profitable.
- Knows the importance of high quality customer service.

It is recommended to promote this person into the position as trainer if possible. If you do not have a certified trainer, then it is recommended to use a manager with the qualities noted above.

You cannot afford to let a non-qualified trainer train your employees. I have been in the business for years and I have seen inadequate training occur in over 75% in the cases.

The worst thing you can do is to let an inexperienced or poorly trained employee train a new person. In my experience, it is an unfortunate event that often occurs; an employee with bad habits or poor training teaches incorrect information to the new staff members. Training is very costly, and you cannot afford to keep hiring, training and losing employees.

This is a domino effect, the non-qualified employee trained someone incorrectly, and the bad habits continue to be passed on as new staff come in. The new person who is poorly trained gets frustrated and either quit or continues the incorrect behavior. This is often referred to as a "rotating door."

As a tool to help you keep the restaurant in the above average area. I would encourage you to empower the trainers to be able to correct any employee that is not following procedures or policies whether they are training or not training. Think of it as a second pair of eyes. To take it further, invite them to participate in the manager meetings. This gives the trainers a strong sense of support and they know their job is an important role in the team.

Server Training
Positive Plus/Corrective Feed Back

Example: While Joe was in the restroom, he overlooked the condition of the restroom; the mirror was dirty, there were no paper towels, and there was trash on the floor.

The manager was up front and saw Joe exiting the bathroom, a few minutes went by and the manager went to the restrooms to tidy them up and saw the condition of the men's restroom.

The Manager cleaned the restroom, the manager spoke to Joe in front of other employee's. He told him that he should not have left the restroom in that condition and he further stated that he was very upset with him.

First of all, you never correct anyone in front of employees or customers. That employee most likely was embarrassed because the manager spoke to him in front of other employees and customers. Do you think that employee will respect that manager? Do you think that employee responded negatively or positively?

Do you think there is another way to get the point across without degrading him or her? I call this process: Positive Plus/Corrective Feed Back

When you have to correct an employee always correct away from other employees and guests. Start the process off with a positive comment.

Explain what needs to be corrected in a positive manner. End the process by explaining why it needs to be done this way.

This is how the manager should have handled it, Joe, I noticed last week you helped out in the dining room and you cleared some tables and swept the floors you did a great job and I appreciate it.

I noticed earlier today that you were in the men's restroom. After you left the restroom I went into the restroom to tidy up, it was not in the best of shape.

In the future will you please make sure you notify me and the dishwasher about the dirty restroom?

Joe, the reason why I need your help is that we don't want the guest to see a dirty restroom that would be a bad impression. Again, I thank you for all your help. Appling this corrective method will give you better results. Think before you say.

In so many cases, managers are not respected for various reasons. The most common reason for that disrespect is how the managers talk to those employees. These types of managers talk to the employees in a degrading manner or disrespectful manner. Treat all employees the same way that you would want to be treated with respect. Communication is a form of art, you need to carefully think before you say, think of several different scenario's along with the outcomes. Choose the best outcome that will give you the best results.

It's a quick fix and the trick to it is to be **fair** and **consistent** with each and every employee.

- Don't be combative.
- Listen to what the employee has to say.
- Think before you speak.
- Come to a conclusion that will work for both you and the employee.
- Sometimes your way is not the best way.

Here is a good example,

Jane was very upset with the manager and the reason for this was the manager sent another employee home without doing any side work. Jane was the closing server and by the manager sending that employee home means who is going to do that employees' side work?

Jane approached the manager and communicated her concerns to him, the manager basically told her that it's her job to finish that side work that the other employee was supposed to do and if she did not like it, then there is the door. You wonder why there is animosity between Jane and the manager.

The manager response should have been "I am sorry I really did not think about the side work not getting done, I will help you complete her side work and in the future, I will make sure if I send someone home early that they complete their side work".

It is all about how we communicate to our staff members and guest along with the way it is delivered. In order to get the respect we have to give respect.

The First Impression are the Guest being Greeted

Greeter Training

The Greeter Position is the most important position in the restaurant, it is the very first impression and if not done consistently and correctly it may create a negative guest experience.

- Greeting the guest is a first priority.
- As the guest enters the restaurant we need to open the front doors for them.
- Great the guest with a warm, sincere smile by saying: hi, welcome to_____ will there be three in your party.
- Seat the guest: immediately when there is an open table.
- Stay within arm's length of the guest as you are seating them.
- Senior citizens: guest with walkers & canes seat up front if possible.
- Tell servers how many guest & what table number.

It is a frequent occurrence in most restaurants that a guest flag down a manager to inform them that the server has not approached them. Seasoned/experienced servers will never let that happen. To be proactive means to head off a potential problem before it occurs. In this instance the hostesses or host can prevent this situation by informing the server that they were just sat. If that server seems flustered or too busy to greet that customer the greeter should immediately advise management.

Management should assign a different server to that table. The manager can approach that table and apologize. The manager can also take a drink order from that table. Use if possible the greeter, they should be trained in order taking.

Under normal situations the greeter needs to inform the server that they were just seated and how many customers are in the group. The greeter needs to watch that table to make sure they are greeted and if for some reason the server cannot make it to that table in time, then the greeter can start the table off with drink orders or inform the manager.

Ultimately, it's the Managers responsibility to be on the floor during all peak times, If you see no silverware on the table, then it's safe to say that they were not greeted.

Greeters should always have in their hands while setting customers, menus and silverware.

Restaurant Greeter Training
Greeter Job Description & Responsibilities

Dress appropriately
- **Males** – Shirts or polo's must tuck in and a belt will be worn (No Jeans)
- Clean-shaven is a must daily, clean khaki or black pressed pants, black non-slip shoes.
- **Females**: Dresses okay, can wear shirts or polo's must be tucked in and a belt will be worn, clean khaki or black pressed pants, black non-slip shoes.

Hygiene
- **Males**: Fingernails trimmed and clean, clean-shaven and hair combed. Tattoos are to be covered up, by using Band-Aids or long sleeve shirts. See management for facial hair guidelines.
- **Females**: Hair that touches the shoulders, needs properly restrained.
- Tattoos are to be covered up, by using Band-Aids or long sleeve shirts.
- Fake nails are not to be worn; nail polish will be neutral in color.

Behavior

- Must be upbeat at all times; always smile when in contact with the customers.
- Respect the customers and staff at all times. No profanity is permitted in the restaurant, especially in the kitchen.
- No drug or alcohol use.

Basic Job Description:

- Arrive to work 5 minutes before the shift begins.
- For communication purposes see the manager prior to starting the shift
- Communicate with the off going greeter for pertinent information about the shift
- The number one priority is greeting the guest as they enter the restaurant.

Part of our **WOW** customer service is to open the door as the guest enters and departs the restaurant. Everyone is responsible in seating the guest. Proper greeting verbiage is the key to good customer service. Greet the guest with a sincerely warm and friendly smile, every time a guest enters our restaurant you will say the following; "Hi, Welcome to "your restaurants name", how many people are in your party today?"

If there are children or infants that require a highchair or booster, always ask, "Would you like a high chair or a booster seat today?" Also, make sure to say hello to the children. Make sure to move chairs if someone is in a wheelchair

Restaurant Greeter Training
Greeter Job Description & Responsibilities

When the guest departs the restaurant, always say: "Thank you for visiting say your restaurant's name and we hope to see you again soon". If your hands full and you physically cannot seat the guest, then acknowledge the guest by saying, "Welcome to, your restaurant's name, someone will be with you shortly," as you are walking in the dining room look for someone who can greet that guest.

The first impression of the guests is how the host or hostess greets them. This first impression is an important part of customer service. Your greeting sets the tone in the customer's mind of whether this restaurant values their guests.

When seating the guest always stay within an arm length of the guest. Walk at the guest pace. Remember that any guest that is disabled or uses a cane or walker that they should be seated up front so the guest does not have to walk far to be seated.

Always offer high chairs and booster seats to families if needed. Make sure that they are clean. High chairs and boosters should be cleaned after a guest leaves the table. The strap to the high chair and boosters should be buckled. This tells anyone that the high chair or boosters have been cleaned.

Menus

- Gather up all menus.
- Clean and sanitize menus and store them in the appropriate area.
- Every time you are on the floor such as, after seating a table or helping out the servers always collect menus.
- If it is not busy then you should help the server's bus & reset the tables.
- Food running is everyone's responsibility.
- If you pass the food pick up window and see food waiting to be delivered, then you should deliver it.

Expediting food to the guest

- Hot food hot & cold food cold
- Proper plate presentation
- Cross check the cook's ticket with what is on the plate to ensure that there is nothing missing.
- Clean plate rims
- Use a plate delivery towel to handle entrée dishes to ensure your hands do not touch the customer's plate.
- Inform the server that you ran the food or offer to assist the server with food delivery.

In some restaurants, servers may have gotten the impression that no one else should deliver the food to the guests, but this is not our philosophy. In reality, there are times the server cannot deliver the food within the ticket standard times because they are too busy greeting the tables, running drinks or other food items, pre-bussing and resetting tables or cashing out the guests. We do not want food sitting in the window waiting to deliver to the guests.

During the peak times, management or food runner need to be in the position of the expo. All employees; management, supervisors, servers, greeters, cooks are responsible for food running. Once the entrees touch the food window, deliver the food quickly.

Other Responsibilities include
- Removing fingerprints from all glass surfaces, front door, display cases etc.
- Sweep vestibule and the front lobby area.
- Keep the lobby area decluttered, clean and organized.
- Check both restrooms on the hour. Utilize restroom checklist. Check whether the paper towels, hand soap, and toilet paper dispensers are full. Use glass cleaner to clean mirrors and sink basins. Check the waste cans and empty when needed. Pick up any debris off the floor. If the toilets or urinals need attention, inform management. Always wash hands after checking the restrooms.
- Cashing the customer out at the front registers.

Cash Handling Procedures

Non POS Registers
There are times that greeter's need to cash out customers at the front registers. When the customer gives you the check to be cashed out, process the check and place the money on top of the money till, do not place the money directly in the money compartments.

Silently count back the change that you are going to give the guest in your mind, then verbally count back the bills and change to the guest. By counting the money twice leaves no room for errors. Once the transaction is completed, then you can place the money from on top of the till into the till. This is to prevent confusion of how much money was given to you.

POS Registers
Open the check by entering the check number or table number into the POS system. Follow the same cash handling procedures above.

Credit Card Procedures

Always make sure you cash the credit card out as a credit card transaction. If you accidently cash out a credit card as a cash transaction you can expect a cash shortage. Simply get a manger to reopen that transaction and cash out the credit card as a credit card transaction.

Always close out all customer transactions immediately. Leaving transactions open in the system after a guest departs the restaurant creates long open table times. Some restaurants track how long customers visit the restaurant by accessing the POS system reports.

These numbers will be skewed by leaving these checks open in the system. Train all employees in the importance of following the correct procedure.

Keep all credit cards slips, private and out of the employees and customers view for security reasons.

The greeter's job responsibilities need to be completed and verified at the beginning of the shift, during the shift and at the end of the shift.

Before leaving for the day or night always have a manager check out your side work.

Employee Signature	Manager Signature	Date

By signing this form you agree to follow all policies and procedures